TRANSMISSIONS

Thanks so much!
Elaine Cosgrove

First published in 2017 by
The Dedalus Press
13 Moyclare Road
Baldoyle
Dublin D13 K1C2
Ireland

www.**dedaluspress**.com

ISBN 978 1 910251 25 6

Dedalus Press titles are represented in the UK by
Inpress Books, www.inpressbooks.co.uk,
and in North America by Syracuse University Press, Inc.,
www.syracuseuniversitypress.syr.edu.

Cover image, 'Triff' by Stephen Salmon,
by kind permission of the artist

The Dedalus Press receives financial assistance from
The Arts Council / An Chomhairle Ealaíon.

TRANSMISSIONS

Elaine Cosgrove

DEDALUS PRESS

TRANSMISSIONS

Elaine Cosgrove

DEDALUS PRESS

CONTENTS

"Spring opens like a blade there."
— Anne Carson, 'The Glass Essay'

"People have a lot more
of the UNKNOWN
than the known in their minds."
— Sun Ra, 'Destination Unknown'

Motorway

It starts as a communication: four trees in an arc-like bow, on a
    hillside in the sun.
Through their branches, a society of brightness—almost pink—
    pierces the bus
and it fills up a cellar lit alive, in a neat second of concrete awe.
    We pass
small towns, big cities, and the immeasurable world, as sure, as
    changeable,
as the scenes that swiftly pass these windows, riding the
    (seemingly) direct motorway.
And as they hurdle by, an overlay of my face stares back—
    wanting to disappear.

Endless

We become adult
on roads, on lines,
on grids, on greens,
on grey spaces —
you cannot zoom in.

We become older
with the city as seer,
decibels the scale
from stepping dawn
to engine rattling dusk,

to clinking night
and walk-back light.
Chiaroscuro lives
in metered hope.

We become in spite
of what happens, and
we are here, still here
becoming with care,
and listening ears.

We become no matter
the distortion that hopes
to confuse our hearts,
and break them.

We become electric.
On and off beings flowing
again and again,
endless in this sudden
glittering world of interruptions.

Eighteen

Cocktails, naggins, and joints—our fodder—
welcome town teenagers thirsty to get wasted
on sour grain, at a house party in LOVELY LEITRIM.

Girl from The Estate stops our taxi and seizes
the sign at the border between counties.
She laughs the whole walk back in the pitch dark

baltic night with the purse of metal under her arm.
A gift of a tall vase from Uncle New York gets broken.
New couples kiss, shift hands on riven couch

under fairy lights. This is our Ballroom of Romance,
in the disused garage. This is our hallowed becoming!
Lough Gill peers up, tired of lewd tunes from the burdened Hi-Fi.

This is our kingdom of youth—forgive us our trespass!
Parke's Castle frowns at us who traipse among
darkened bluebells in the forest behind the house.

We want to hold, and chat to the fairies' stones.
'Let them listen to us,' we say, touching their moss.
'Yeah,' those who grow here say, 'Let them hear it.'

Let them know the shoddy stories caused by spell
of their garland lights, our dwelling, joints, and gin.

Bass Guitar

E.
My first—a cheap one bought in Cranmore—was stolen
from the Trades Club by boyos on speed with too much time.
Leon saw some of its flesh-like shrapnel on Rockwood Parade.
But my second, *the second one*—a Phil Lynott black P-bass
(mirror plate) to go with leather pants, and cat-kohl eyes—
    played magic.

A.
The stage lights blow up: splinter-flash on racks of young faces.
Heart's chambers boom in The Ambassador; bass clef springs
    alive.

D.
Lunchtime—April Saturday—in a high-rise block. Partner holds
    a hammer
outside locked spare single room. Polish kids play with their new
    words
on the green. The ice cream van comes around, *Match of the Day*
    jingles.
The hammer-man is having a panic attack. The pinna in her ear
    waits
for the bang cracking the rosewood frets, the maple neck, the
    alder body.

G.

Fifties Hits, parents' bedroom and nothing-to-do summer Saturdays.
The house all to my sister and me dancing on imaginary street
    corners
of American diners. *Dax*-hair and over-sized shirts mimic the
    steel-pluck
of speaker strings. The doo-wop purity of *Only you, Only have
    eyes for you,*
In the still of the night, Blue Moon, Earth Angel is satin in the pits
    of our stomach.

Cruinniú

They look at me, a strange Marconi of Sligo-learnt Irish,
as I tap, tap transcribe *a gcuid smaointe* onto flipchart
in a nursing home's rosewater day room.

The old people here—some returned labourers from Leeds,
some homemakers who never left—use different words to mine.
Theirs is Irish older than I can imagine; *teanga* as they know it.

I use the topic THE CORAL STRAND as icebreaker and what Mag says
under her breath to the Muintir an Tí I don't catch
but they're laughing hysterically now. *Cad é?* I ask. Young anxiety

flint-reddener to my throat. She translates the laughter line:
'The Devil's Balls is what we call The Coral Strand'
and they are fits of giggles again—a formation melting stiff air.

As we work, Mag instructs me when I drop a fada by accident.
She picks up slipped schooling while the lady-to-her-left clicks wool.
She tells me: 'Don't put a fada over that *ú* in *ghuth*', so I scribble
    it out.

How does the water feel in their memory; how large does it appear?
Their kestrel-brown school pinafores attempt to lift at their hems
with sharp swerve of the rolling Atlantic breeze.

Their bare feet might have pecked the thick broken band of
    maerl shells
until they reached the skate-smooth rock pools. It is icy-tropical
    blue
at The Coral Strand. White marble in grey interior. So blue, so blue.

Pure bolstered, I ask if they'd like anything different?
The quietest lady in the group pipes up. We all turn to look.
Moss welly of group's only man hovers silently as hobby over
    linoleum.

'Brown bread,' the lady says and the man nods.
'Brown bread with my tea would be nice.' *Arán donn* inks the
    board.
Smiles break over their faces. Teeth, white crests meeting in old
    gold cove.

Surfing at Streedagh Strand

Site of a Spanish Armada wreckage, Sligo

During sea-salt of winter surf, remembrance
of lineage acts like zinc on the blood that swells
from a creviced nick beside my thumbnail.

Streedagh Strand pulls out her linen towel
and I become warm dough on the sea floor
when their bodies appear blood-strewn bits on grain.

Five hundred wiped-out sailors beat, robbed and stripped
ashore by local savages hungry for wealthy bones
and soaked goods falling like crumbs from their dying.

A good savage attending only to castles and mountains
De Cuellar said of O'Ruairc who gave the Spaniards
fresh-cut reeds to sleep on, rye bread to eat

in the Breffni mountains where they hid.
My soft hands roughen to withstand whip of board,
cold knife in December tide earthing me straight to the skin.

The Crossing

'Sea broke on land to full identity'—Seamus Heaney

Their black rescue dinghy
came desperate, shuddering onto the shore,
came an orange lifejacket in flight to Lesbos

shivering a first point of safety on an unspeakable map
that yields to an ebb, to a soft crash leaping
from sea-salted rubber to warm sand, hands scooping

it up thanking *Allah* for their luck. Each drew a breath
before the next chapter—and us, the far away, swiped
tearful eyes knowing what waited for them further inland.

Handwrapping

Eventually, you learn to wrap the cloth your own way.
First by imitation—online videos by peers, Master's
and partner's real-life instructions. *What feels assured
is what you come to make yourself.* The snugger the wrap
to experience, the stronger the hand's form, just before the strike.

Lime

Lime is the cordial.
Lime is the kiln.

Lime is the white stones
that makes fields grow.

Lime is the green heart
on a woven bracelet.

Lime is the neon on a copybook
of my *Aisling* education.

Lime is a bad decision tank top,
leg warmers and Grunger tee.

Lime is the fruit of fun, a segment
highlighting the important stuff.

Lime is a painted door, hammer, steel.
Lime is a dash on night-after-night out.

Pluto

Sleep shut, I am trying to get back to Pluto.
It is a world climbed to through a tree house
that is sat within a grand tree planted, found
at a junction of grim, grey littered primary roads.
I've forgotten the sentence that gets me back.

I don't know what to do or who to ask for help.
I'm left to try to recall in an ugly flat down the road.
I stay inside because those who walk outside are violent,
I am frightened by their bad intent. So, I sit
in a forfeit pew and wait, turn my teeth,
skin sore for resilience to resurface.

It's so beautiful there, on Pluto.
It's a garden of golden, soughing lines,
glorious charm that makes you smile all the time.
I wait for the code—the jigsaw trick—
I wait for the magic of remembering it.

Afterglow

The paper says the bees are dying
without pollination—

They can't suckle flora and cause sneezes,
valentines, funerals, weddings, apology gifts
and 'get well soons'.

They're dressing up for death,
killed by safe seekers' pounding hands.

Be gone little buzz, be gone on dutiful,
couple occasions.

To see faces of them burning back into life,
day after day,
was afterglow—magnificent.

Be gone, little buzz, be gone.
They're dressing up for death.

Keeping It Under Wraps

Rejoice the opportunity
to engage in the morning commute.
Rejoice the day for the privilege
to authenticate the greyscape
with browblack caffeine.

What do you think of when
you close your eyes?
Is it the person you desire?
Bed's warmth, cosy as a shell,
cold metal zips, undressing?

Do you depict the radical job
that you know gut-sure you would adore?
Are you reviewing the souvenir
of a flawless event?

Shhh   (If you can hear it)

It's the loudness of your heart
beating the big band's arrival,
ushering happiness in.

White Paper

What was it?
It's being lying here for weeks,
this poem, unwritten
and ruling the back of my mind.
White paper—for what?
Something I read. Something
I probably liked the sound of,
but memory houses short tendencies.

Instead, in white paper's place
will be the boats in the harbour,
the music man by my side who
encapsulates my shivering body
with a coat of morning talk,
us sitting at the early house—
fooled late morning explorers
gum-hooked on speed.

Yen

Too much sugar makes hives.
The processed stuff, the instant hit:
It gives you itchy legs.

You need to move, you need to bug,
you need to get it out of your system.

You need healthy back in there to run
smooth as a kite tacking on sea salt air.

You need the bluster blur of cars
banging past on a town road
to act as a backdrop to the scene
of yourself
heliolatric and bijou,
still as a painter's portrait hanging out
on time you've made organically.

No one is expecting a deadline;
they are in silent mode profile.

You're on chosen self-sufficient means.

Cave of Forgotten Dreams

after the Werner Herzog documentary of the same title

These are some of our modern remains;

I.
Good milk pours from a carton three-quarter full,
down the sinking of odd mornings lurching in a mother's gut
as her son's car swings out—sprays gravel—to buy cigs.

II.
White paper slip stuffed into a brown envelope
by man in red, arm-striped tracksuit. Swollen face,
an outburst of tears, PRESS BUTTON exits the dole office.

III.
Perfume-free body lotion—the thick emulsion—paints
on to dead dry skin of a next-of-kin's examinations.
UV light burns off stress scales in the hospital.

IV.
White knuckles in a transit van marriage. Cymbals crash
down a dusty argument. Death high silences ring;
ear-marked and discriminated futures don't pan out.

V.
Silver mints tumble red lipstick, a rushed smoke,
a kiss hello. Arm and breath around her shoulders.
Blushes settle like weights in a Galilean thermometer.

VI.
White strip light common room, waiting room,
red ruled feint page. Headlamps pick out winter heads
yellow and damp. Travel lines slip-stitch, walking home.

Outside the 24hr

First we all hear the shuffling noise.
Look! a tourist outside Spar exclaims—her phone,
a pitchfork claim, a *scamall* despair, our local newsprint's
state stories so close, they rumble, and they ignore it.

The Ex points his finger up at 'Another person gone with the
    river.'
Oh, Friday hearts sink, desk-minds about their business.
Turning around, he said it again, tilting his callous cigarette,
and moved on to the pub.

It is confirmed by a stranger. 'Yup, it's rescue.'
We stand looking skyward, circular pattern tracking.
Tapping the PIN with one hand, the other clutching rib.
The couple outside Spar, passers' gawking steps,

the rotors' babble-cut blades in my purse,
palm hover, cover the PIN, screen instruct user,
the noise creeps over necks tilted too many times for comfort.
And I want to turn my head too. Up, away

to nose the noise as it goes over building tops,
as sure as flight paths, as saddening as the river flow.
Taking the money from the slot's silver mouth,
I snap it in between the lock too close to our bones.

'Rescue for nothing,' he says. No. Rescue is everything.

Sonnet

What does the failed heart know anymore?
Does it know to live on until it dies;
to stop being a balled-up fury
of wringing hands that bathe in salt to wrinkles?
What does the breaker know of the lupine days
paid for on a three-bedroom flat minus one,
minus you? Canary-coloured walls ear
the bounce-back of silence over dinner.
What does the connection do when it's gone?
How do the lines fill up their hollow gaps
with new wires? Will the feedback from the
permanent interruptions make you turn off the sound?
 This from your breaker: learn to make
 a joy that's all your own and make it very loud.

A Stab at Love

Spirits gather at 4 a.m., the evening before November.
His friend says she aspires to be in a relationship like ours.
He—my man—doesn't look at me but at the floor
between his gapped-tooth hands, replies politely, 'Thanks.'

I'm delighted she said it, but I sense he's feeling guilty
for the past taking stock. Black marble mute as my voice
condensates under settling pints. Plastic silver starlets flash
save me save me from this bar we should head home from.

Home to words that bump out in the after-hour.
Home to the fall-out from his separation.
Home before they bitter our popped-rock tongues.
Home to tears at a loss to a brush-drum rattle.

Maybe I should have said instead to his friend
that I try to go with the everyday stuff: a kiss, a runic smile,
the touch t-minus to the normality of his presence;
the metallic constellation of his van keys thrown on the kitchen
    table.

Rumi with Shams

Every time a country song comes on the radio,
I'm sure we're going to crash Coen Brothers-style.

But it's never happened
so allow me to be a bit more serious:

A forecast for doom is in your transit—
is in your up-and-leaving all the time.

Smoking Area

This maroon interior is bald due to sitter's strokes,
and mahogany wood sanitised too many times.

I should know better than pretend to be naïve
to talk dropped like beer mats under a round.

I go out to smoke, for a break, but every toke
is a question mark rising in a hot air balloon.

Anatomical

Outside the window, outside where solid ice heaps make
hyaline tunnels for trapped bicycles, where glass bottles poke
out their heads, where winter hiccups, where summer sucks in
too much; girl's throat is buttercup, lemon, mustard, rapeseed,
canary, dun, and cocoa holding cacophonic breath in vain.
Bye-bye *crunch, crunch,* shreds and feet glee. Hello, World! to
girl who thinks she is woman, who puts her hand to his face
where it is stubbly then smooth as she moves her hand across
his cheek, trotting over his jawbone with her fingertips, onto
the valley of his neck, filling in the wait for his waking-up.
She sees the U-Bahn like a victorious sprinter to the ribbon
line—how commuters at Heuston dart out from the columns
on sight of the Luas pulling up. Lamps cross-dissolve to black
spots before eyes, thrilling. She rests her hand where lines made
from a longer life than hers elbow for space on gaps between
his fingers which have known a life lived in three more cities,
in more shared flats, in more relationships that had been happy
but had ended abruptly. Does it need to break to become anew,
or is it aftersun comfort in banal disaster? Picking at a spot on
her back, she turns over onto her side, bringing his hand with
her. Ask her what she feels like today and she will lie. It will
be *Oh, I'm fine Oh, I'm grand* mumbling starling mouths for
cheerfulness. No cerulean, teal, or royal explanations. It's not
exactly a secret; it is difficult to say, to broadcast in the secretive
city of the heart. And this is it in her mind's grid: a smallness
gung-ho, avoiding blush-mortifying shame; taking note of
pigments to stay the whitewash.

Systole, Diastole

Black mood is back and porous.
Redford face: a carved cold cave. This night,
you cannot find any comfort in sleep.
Clutter-thoughts climb ventricles:
systole they contract,
diastole they expand. Hunger reverberates.
Systole composition, *diastole* slumbers and wakes.
Systole rubbish-heap in backfield, on landfill,
all over street. *Diastole* potting landscape daydreams
when you cannot find any comfort in sleep.
Systole lower into strata, *diastole* into earthworms,
into fungi, into other bodies that reside within.
Systole composition, *diastole* Blue-eyed Shag
that dives a plumage of black clouds into ocean.
Comes back still dry; icy catch in beak alight.
This night, when you cannot find any comfort in sleep
systole composition, my dear,
diastole little niche in soil found.

Doon Lough

I go to Doon Lough
and wait for my head to clear. I plank out
my legs—revel in some sweet doom metal sounds.

An archaeologist informs me last week
they found the oldest known remains
in Leitrim, in a cave, south of Fawnary Hill.

Strange score of young boy's shards
paused in process through time for their return.

Carried to dark mouth, left in dry vessel
for his flesh to fray like bark from his white bones.

They left him there—mysterious misfortune
never brought to his final place.
Instead, he dissolved and trickled down with the stones.

He might be a man now feeding the wild and regulated.
From here to the water, he is the sedge fly breathing ripples.
He is protector of Doon Lough. He is the presence that consoles.

Reservoir

Some
of the
reservoir
workers
were
my people
in
New York,
building
to bring
clean
water
to
the
city.

My
people
lived
in
the
black
water's
depths,
inverted
inherited
reservoir
megalithic
tombs
dissecting
Hudson
River
plateau.

Valve
chambers
were cold
smelts
of
Gile
and
gravity
resisting
depths
in
the
Rondout.

Break
of
black
blue
water
cold
out
in
valve
chamber;
an
equation
of
a minus
heart
and
plus
city
stop.

They
work
in the
depths,
my people
the immigrants
who build
the
city,
alive
alive
I
AM
ALIVE
in
the
pits.

The
equation
abstracts
the
homes,
multiples
the
city
with
clean
water
for
each—
and—
all
to
drink
from
and
behold.

Bog Disco

It should have been the old bloomeries of love
during the slow-set: disco lights like Morse Code baubles
roaming our sequins, skirts and shirts
but some smart aleck two plastic, parish seats away from me
belches and says: 'Boom. It's the erection section.'
So I make tracks swift, double-door into a true breather of a night.
The Plough, dazzling points floating in the sky.

His Work Lives On

for Louis MacNeice, Poet and BBC Sound Effects Collector

Too wet to be out on the moors.
What a necessary fool, but Ha!
I love his commitment to task.
His clothes stuck to his bones—
he'll catch his death, and he did.

What he records is everywhere
he egressed. From fieldwork,
for sake of airplay's intention—
for our ears to make visible what eyes

cannot see. Twist of recorder, variation
of water's flow on stone, *drop drop drop*
to well's end. Listeners will never know
his plans for those effects. The damp, oily
sheet a cover, an incubator for last healthy breath.

When I close my eyes, I hear
a gorgeous playful palace of noise
and see snug in a vault the rows
of odd comfort from cataloguing the unknown.

Cupid's Text Arrow

Outside my front door, before I scramble for my keys,
I have to get this message sent. I lean slanted
against my housemate's car, a sad spade not in use.

Using both eyes and thumbs to guide me,
'I think I like you'. Signed. Sent. Delivered.
Characters' dart towards the wonder of the semantic.

Then, my grip loses the phone and it splats, innards
everywhere. When I plunge over to teddy-pick them,
I nosedive. A pancake flipped onto frost-spiked grass, giggling.

Spongy

Kids skid on the first day ice.
Nail tips trace sleet flakes as they fall.
Salt drops make bespoke goggles and sleet turns 3-D.
A lonely feeling is kneeling on stomach lining,
swashbuckling to nerve-ends *chevaux-de-frise*
on another day of typing at computer
half nine to one, two to half five.

A passenger hits the STOP bell.
Feet to pavement, canals covered, off to destination
in nimbus sound-worlds.
Monday to Friday it's just her and the screen
discussing the lives of marginalised women.
They have voices, but upstairs is too busy talking
the appropriate jargon that will package facts into stories.

Her CV reads: involved, 'good capital',
a type searching for the post-whatever
because the present isn't ever enough.
The truth is somewhat pathetic. She marks out a volley
of raining tears, shingles onto the sink, the mouse-mat, the notepad.
A *tap, tap, tap* telegram that she has not been well for a while
but, who's listening? Who is really listening when we arrive?

The Concrete Line

7:10 a.m.—the line under us.
We laugh: we both wore purple today.
15 Window
16 Aisle
2 Bewley's coffees, white napkins
1 beheaded sugar packet
2 stick stirrers and a banana ready in my hand.

Sluggish chat about the meeting ahead.
I unpeel the banana and offer you some.
Approaching Athenry station.
The WC sign is on,
my phone beeps in 2/4 telegraph timing.

Approaching Athenry station.
I take the phone from my coat pocket—
a message from your boyfriend
to say your beautiful sister
just passed away.

Sleepy cows, one light bungalow,
bare trees, the black *chug chugs* by.

Clips from an Old Apartment

They decorated it with photo frames; small motifs of spent
　occasions
chequered about, stood up, laid down in polka, rust, wood and
　plastic.

There was a large bed, there, for her to set her things down onto
　black & white
cotton sheets. Lucid mornings, leaves outside were shadow
　puppets in the reel,

elegant dancers on primrose wall. Divisive mornings, slack arrest
　with curtains drawn.

Sunday legs walk in-line on the Promenade; his fingers ascend
her Kirby-grip embrace, pause for digital square to freeze them
　in stop-caught smiles.

Gloved hands slap. Port lips kiss. Vanilla-musk and rose liquorice
　he bought
adds scent to disowning notions of a couple of kids, a mortgage,
　a car, a dog.

She goes along with his plans for too long, they say in passing.
　She waits to find
the right time. Once safe, she sets out with a quiet beacon under
　her arm.

Two Guys

I climb through air vents
avoiding conversation
on knee to palm to knee engrams,
afraid the world might not like my gush
of preference, my smile when it falls through.
The guy I fancy, the one who gives me paper clip legs
and a board of impressions I'd like to shift;
he's not the one who will bring me one true sentence.
Fancy looks scarily good enough to eat the words I scaffold,
to pen-mark out of ten our interactions, mind-map thoughts on
                                                    the taste
of our acquaintance, feel the freeze of nerves jamming. He looks
                                        good but shakes
voice. He sandpapers my muscles up. He's the kind of guy who
                                would encourage my hand
if I wanted to toss a smoke bomb to leave no presence. And If I
                                vanished, I'd reappear on a
comfy couch for a tasty smoke with my beamnote friend where
        we would research, side-by-side, ideas for our futures. Led Zep
        frisking out the decibels with Custard Pie, and *down by the
        seaside all the ships go sailing by.* I could road trip with him
        until our buddyship runs out of fuel, at the end of the line.
        Around him, I'd stay out. I'd stay delightfully outside
                                        of myself.

Night Bus with Headphones

Dark night passenger
Dark night the drum-beat
Dark night in ears, the fader crossing into keep
Dark night alleys, dark night towns
Dark night tired-eyes of morning moving
Dark night down the Swanee
Dark night levees of sleet break
Dark night window wipers oscillate.

Dark night flash of figures in camera
Dark night where lovers meet
Dark night tint in frontier
Dark night of the soul dissipates:
Dark night with *sun, sun, sun.*

Nightcall

They have their calls—the gulls,
and I have mine to make this evening.
Plaintive prelude of *keows, mews,*
alarms to the fall of night,
their fish-want cries, territories,
mates, laser beams darting
across the resting sky.

I twitch my cigarette out the window
as a cat might do when it simply listens,
ears equally twitching, starving for a hand
to reach out a plate and place it down in front,
or as it might in the lead-up to the push of hunt,
or as it might when a flea is in need of solving.

Emoticon

The high ones die, die. They die. You look up and who's there?
What would Berryman's Mr. Bones think of this:
the use of smiley faces? They're all out in the Club.
Sometimes, they make me want to gag face
but I click-colon-bracket and watch television
after midnight, wearing an excellent and delicate mask.

The Loop

I do not want to cross it
but I know I must
with this egg-sized shape in me.

I do not want to cross them
but I know I must
with borrowed cash,

borrowed case from unknowing dearness.

I do not want to cross
with this carry-on—
attempt to pack all thoughts

into less than yellow bar of 26 x 53.

I do not want to cross him
but I know I must
as the flight takes path

little ice lights blink in rhythm across the sea,
the loving sea, green sea that banishes me.

Leeds, Liverpool, London,

I do not want to cross these cities at all
but I know I must in secrecy
declare passport, heart gushing with want

to ask them, do you know I will be safe?
Do you know to the taxi-man, to the nurse,
to the magazine in this eggshell blue waiting room.

Firemen Waiting

Shutters are up on front of station—engines gleam, exposed.
Two firemen puck a sliothar to pass time
in the half-time between emergencies.
The ball rises, thick stitched moon over traffic light, red.
The pure boldness of these responsible men, spilling out over
the curbs—their sniggers at a tugged warning from an older one
who waters sweetpea plants on the station's windowsills:
'Careful on that road, lads,' as he tilts the typical green can.
Autumn's air wraps her hands around us—dice of delicacy
under wire, coil, tank, hose. Chill will come, and we'll always
know this. Hear their attention in the green dip, the go of sirens—

Banana Phoblacht

March 2006

Let the lights dim low and bellow softly.
Let colour diffuse into atoms of box-flat
and dehydrated speckles of off-whiteness.

Let the smoking ban be abolished
and let smoke flicker to engulf the atmosphere
until it stings water out from our eyes.

Let Tom Waits appear out of the kitchen corner
through slapping doors to play
his bloodorehematite scales, and announce

to customers that the piano really
has been drinking. Let a man sit and stare
at her near empty glass, latte cup and be enthralled

by the trace of sodapink lipstick tracked
around the rim. Let him think of her slicking it on
before they met.

Let this scene be assassinated
and spliced as he rubs his neck,
stands, gathers his coat and leaves.

Spine Breaker

You hated when I borrowed your books.
The books you carried from Hartlepool to Hull,
Cardiff to London, to Galway. There was I tramping thumbs
over ex-girlfriend's delicate fingers and breaking their linen backs.

It's better, I think, to look like you've been enjoyed,
rather than kept for the mint condition.
I just hated it when the book flopped too much to the right
or to the left and I couldn't concentrate on the words.

Hush and Fall Asleep to Fantasy

I'm kicking glass on a city that is white shirt
washed-out bare on a race night

where I'm annoyed at our West for
mashing chips into the cobbled streets,

picking up littered hearts that shout somatic
are ya single, ya fookin' ride?

I hear them through my skylight, I hear them
through my skylight on Lower Dominick Street;

their heels wet with men's piss
from the two o'clock beauty parade

jolting us wide awake in our bedrooms
to the haw of cigarettes lighting up off of ash,

shoes sole-slicking tanned bags
and chip shop vomit,

Girls who wear assholes' ties around their necks
like ponies with medallions riding their clobber towards
the voyage home, taxi-less.

Kilometres, hours away in your memory
foam bed, does its making remember the twist

of my waist against your back making the snug for bedtime?
The nudge of resin hips slow dancing in your kitchen
to Submarine songs?

The neglect we give to Galway on Ladies Day;
the trade-in on those Brassaï heart-stoppers.

This is the apocalyptic discipline we give over
on a vision of 'class' for one day

choking for the *fake it, make it* party time
white shirt washed-out bare without a lampshade,
without a face wipe;

make-up creased into lines that say I'm fucked, forgive me!
I wanted to hear your voice down the line announcing

the drums are at it again: taking ba-deap, ba-dap flights
on a flicker board reading 'Atlantic-side window'

falling into a slip of unconsciousness,
into the liking for another kiss.

You know, I'd pop-up a PA system on Shop Street,
unfurl a velour cloth motive, use the shop fronts

to Rubik cube re-structure an Ella Fitzgerald style café,
stop all the pissheads and nitrate them so that

I could stand on top of the bars of a rickshaw buggy
and sing to you this megaphone wish:

Let's do it, let's fall in love.

Arms

I wake up, parched,
with a black cat
at my feet,
and Guinness like glue
in my gut.

The other mouser's
paws stair-creep—
a lean shadow
behind blinds
half-drawn in dusk.

The way
that rain
pelts down
the roof—
it's rough.

I am too old
for this house's
strange sounds
to cause such alarm.
I am too attached

to the spoon
of strong arms in the night.
Blacklion's checkpoint
breaks.
Woollen heads,

hollow eyes
and guns from TV

flood over—
Faces so imprecise
you cannot see them

from the window
without light.
Only the white
of their eyes shine
when they get too close.

Riding the Blue L

The grid of Chicago
in the snow-stomped lines
of a worker's boot.

Cocktail

At first, they were beautiful.
An exotic box of cocktail colours,
an array of keen aims for night.

The more I drew their pretty heads in,
the more I offered them out to strangers
stuck for conversation. Passer byes were amused.

They started to question the exquisite smokes.
I started to question myself—the tilt and shake
of Magenta notions, burning brightly off my hand.

I grew wary of them, but went on
until the box was done. My smokes,
we have come full circle.

I suck the last grey out of your golden tip,
celebrate its grim headstone on my lips,
chuck it to the pavement:

'G'luck to you, and Goodnight.'

Listless Day in Town

The road to hell is paved with good intentions

Gold. Nothing is ever easy.
We carry places within us.
Collect 1,000 points
if you buy *Coconut Shy*.
Smells nice and cheap
as my previous men smelt
iron ore bills and paperwork.
Insurance. Get insurance
when I am thirty-five.
Oh, how I may manipulate
myself on Hair Styling apps.
Whiten my teeth just in case
I die with stained teeth.
Clouds. Grids. New contact
lenses. Automatic renewal.
Omnipresent repairs. Am I using
my money for what exactly?
Oh, my history of credit. I see.
All my fixed assets are depreciating.
Better stop social smoking.
Funeral casket crosses my mind.
Portfolios and yellow wallpaper.
Put it on and see how it fits, please.
It looks nice on you. It's only 13 euro.
Glossy white perpetual floors, perpetually browsing.

Visitor

And they stop to raise their heads to look skyward
to where the guide's finger points and the church
is where it is pointing
And the older woman—the visitor—looks instead
at a pose of younger women who come towards her,
and she smiles at them, greets them, 'Good Morning',
in an American accent
And they smile back, and giggle, and walk
And this woman's graceful expression is so damn luminous
I cannot help but stare from the café's doorway while I wait.
And you know from her very gait, she is one who devotes
her whole being, whole life, to the pursuit of kindness.
And as if to prove this thought, she raises her left hand—
frail and pretty—to where the guide had pointed
and says to her husband: 'Imagine! We're as old as that.'
And she stands, smirking up at it, looking proud.

No. 64

Stalled
in this holy bogland—
KNOCK AIRPORT.

Northwest Radio county
custard cake scored
from mounds of asphalt

and heaps of car park
spaces
on rain-wet lines.

Up here,
the mountains'
peaty shoulders

are guardians
for landing,
departing passengers.

In town, lowly Eircom
telephone kiosks

are ten-cent-checked
by rolly-stained
fingers,

stout-breath
supplemented
marriages,

and 1981-style
horseshoe boxed
hedges.

I think about him,
luck and boxes.

Will my old ones
precipitate made-up minds?

I think:
why does it still matter
anyhow?

We don't need every
tradition to punctuate
all decision.

I think about
new beginnings
with him.

It isn't sweet tractors
rotting rubber wheels
into the ground.

It is work-ready wheels
fertilising weeds
outside magnolia houses.

No Responsibility,

to make me gag with laughter.
No responsibility to be a Department 8
affair. To be your Delta of Venus.
But how I want to make you come
to my apartment, to my bed,
to get whatever's going on between us
out. No responsibility to be burlesque,
to explode. *Shoo shoo*, out
so we can go on living
with the ones we're meant to be with.
So I can stop dream-setting you—
your hands to your head on the ground
to a mash-up of The Ronettes *be my baby*
and the Joker's *why so serious?*
No responsibility to be dutiful to lust
that palpitates. You take a bus out of town
to leave me stranded at the first stop.
You never tell me that you're going back,
and I forget to look around.

Giant's Causeway

It is the sum
of its parts

It is pools from rainfall

It is the summer
of my smiles

It is selected memories
of an impression
of a volcanic eruption

It is the sum
of its parts

It is the springtime
of my loving

of an impression

It is domes
depressions
glittering
columns
salt crystal
hollows

It is basalt
that is your hair

It is the organ
of my fingertips
touching

greys,
dark greys,
blacks, browns

It is the sum
of its patient parts
of a joyful impression

*These are the seasons
of emotion*

It is every minute
changing light

It is graceful mercy
of what is
shed upon it

It is delight
in a disorder
of symmetry

*Wonder
of devotion*

It is recognition
to its making

It is a presence
It is small details

It is the sum
of its parts

It is this hope
a causeway
that outflows

It is the *little rain
that falls*,
out to the sea.

Greening

The life in us is like the water in the river .... It may rise this year higher than man has ever known it, and flood the parched uplands.
— Henry David Thoreau, Quote at St. Vincent Plaza, Little Rock, AR

I.

Cold February, Galway Novena comes around again.
Students burst home past the Cathedral's line.
The rain starts to come down hard and under white flap,
a trailer is a serendipitous sheltering where I browse tin-silver
Mary-embellished bracelets, medals and rings.

A woman walks, a Titian blue cardigan like nun's habit turned
    inside out,
drenched to her hair. The holy-swag seller, a man devoid of chat,
    has his hands
crossed like the reposed. His hands are a weathered Islander's:
    waxy, tanned
with chubby tips. His hands marked by buried welts from oars
    and pony-strap traps
draw me back to an afternoon in a split-house in South Gaines
    Street, Little Rock—

Back to questions of repair, of pining and of the attached—
back to minding a strangeness—back to the kill-heat
of an August in Arkansas, back to the taxi ride from the airport,
back to letting myself in, back to the want for a shape on things.

II.

It was a mutual friend at a wedding, due to return.
It was new conversation and the surprise of a person when least
    expected.
It was the mention of an important name: his friend deceased
who smiles broadly in several wooden frames. His kindness,
    phosphenes
off his tongue. His smile, a stacked skyline among sacred heart
    idols.

The dead man's wife got many holy tokens over the years from
    friends,
he explained. I told him about the white trailers that sell bric-á-
    brac during the Novena—
little slots filled with beliefs and hopes. Trailers that sell—the rest
    of the year—
chips, cans, crisps and burgers at matches, concerts, beaches and
    sides of roads.
I told him about a Virgin Mary ring that left a weed-green band
    around the base

Of my middle finger when I was young.
Copper made green out of oxygen and acids.
Green made out of summer sports sweat,
washed hands, peas of rose-perfumed creams.

III.

His drawl spoke towards his hand
where a knuckle was bumpy from use of a Beveller's hammer.
He told me more about the passing: brain tumour, twenty-nine.
Could I reach out then and softly rub his hand with mine?
The dead heat came in again so, we sat out on the porch

For the slant breeze off the fan. Ankles-up on the ledge;
punch cans like blue-and-white statues on our laps. The cicadas
    click
in the trees on South Gaines Street; the fan's rotation was the sound
of a Thoreau river flow. This damned Galway rainwater is a jug
    knocked
over the awning's edge. The trombone of the Longview train
    breaking the night

At 3 a.m. in Little Rock is now a beeping car where I am, at home.
Hands work to sand rough edges clean.
And as the clouds spill out, cold February, a whet for warmth,
and the seams of love, tug and flood, turning everything green.

Home

from the festival

       z
     z
   z
He is Z beside me
a rise and fall
of ribcage.

He is too humble,
too loyal to be
assigned E-U-S.

Nonetheless,
he is my god
in this scenario.

He does not stir
to my arrival,
which I am a bruised
peach about—
all acquired ego,
from the poets.

I am home, love,
ready to graft
my way out
of the talk-shop.

I want to jab his side
with my finger,
and command

an alt universe
for us,

'Rise and fall
to the woman
of your dreaming.'

Instead, he smells
like a brewery
and I fen,
a half-naked sliver

                    s

              s

        s
of tiredness,
touch-screening
white light keys
of Notepad,
as it extends
and shines upon
his face and arms,
my face too—

a flickering
          tap tap
hold down
          transform
letter
          suggest
          autocomplete
flicker
          tap
flicker

      tap
return
      tap
return
      tap
return
      hold
      flicker
lightning
connect
socket
      charge
wake up   scoop up
my body   become
my peering   point

NOTES

p.14 *cruinniú*   meeting

   a gcuid smaointe their thoughts

   teanga   tongue

   Cad é?   What's that?

   muintir an Tí   residents

   ghuth   voice

   An dtuigeann sibh chuid gCearta? Would you understand your Rights?

   arán donn   soda bread

p. 29 shams – collective noun slang for people who drive their cars recklessly for thrills

p. 34 Gile – mythological figure who lived in the bottom of Lough Gill, Co. Leitrim

p. 47 Banana Phoblact – café that used to be in Galway City, since closed-down

p. 57 'No. 64'– the route number for the Galway to Sligo to Derry bus

p. 59 *Delta of Venus* – book of erotic short stories by Anaïs Nin

p. 60 Lyrics from 'Rain Song' by Led Zeppelin in italics

p. 67 peering points: term used to describe voluntary interconnection between two points—e.g. two networks—for mutual benefit.